Copyright © 2024 João Castro
All rights reserved.
ISBN: 9798346281771

Table Of Content

Introduction: Welcome To The World Of Ai-Powered Development — 1

Chapter 1: Embrace Your Inner "Idiot" — 5

Chapter 2: Getting Started With Ai Tools — 8

Chapter 3: Building Your First Plugin — 16

Chapter 4: Designing Your First Template — 23

Chapter 5: Automation Made Simple — 33

Chapter 6: Testing, Troubleshooting, Optimization, And Security — 41

Chapter 7: Deployment And Launch — 49

Chapter 8: Expanding Your Skills — 57

Chapter 9: Improving Site Performance And Seo — 67

Chapter 10: Easy Deployment And Maintenance — 76

DEDICATION

To every challenge that tested me and every late-night Google search that turned me from a curious learner into a self-taught tech enthusiast, developer, and design lover. To family, the ultimate motivation, and to the thrill of doing what I love—even if it all began with a necessity, a lot of persistence, and a touch of desperation. For every line of code that nearly had me throw in the towel, there was always a reminder: I'm here because I'm stubborn, self-driven, and maybe a little obsessed with solving problems and creating beautiful things.

Thank you, life, for the curveballs, and thank you to every bug and design flaw that forced me to dig deeper. It's all part of the journey, and honestly, I wouldn't have it any other way.

Introduction: Welcome to the World of AI-Powered Development

Hello, fellow creators, entrepreneurs, and tech enthusiasts! I'm João Castro, a passionate web developer with over 17 years in this wild, ever-evolving world of tech. I'm here to let you in on a little secret: you don't have to be a coding prodigy to turn your ideas into reality. With the right AI tools, you can build plugins, design templates, and create beautiful, functional websites without becoming fluent in JavaScript or PHP. In fact, all you really need is an idea, a bit of curiosity, and a willingness to explore. I'll show you the rest.

Maybe you're an artist, an entrepreneur, or simply someone with a great idea and no coding background. If that's you, then 1% Developer, 99% Idiot! is designed just for you. This book is my way of saying that WordPress development isn't just for hardcore coders; it's for anyone with a vision, a spark, and the right tools to bring it to life. With AI by your side, you can fast-track from idea to execution without drowning in technical jargon or waiting for a developer to bring your concepts to life.

Why This Book?

Throughout my career, I've seen countless people brimming with creative ideas but feeling blocked by the maze of technicalities involved in bringing them to life. These people have vision—they know what they want their site to do, how it should feel, and maybe even what it should look like. But when it comes to actually building it, the world of code seems overwhelming, the learning curve steep, and the costs of hiring a developer daunting.

This book is here to change that narrative. I wrote it because I believe that you can be a "1% developer"—the one who brings the creative ideas, the vision, and the courage to dive in, while letting AI handle the heavy lifting. This isn't a book to make you a master coder; it's a guide to help you take control of your ideas and bring them to life faster and with fewer hurdles, all while exploring a new way of thinking about tech and creativity.

What You'll Find in This Book

This isn't a typical coding manual; it's a toolkit for using AI to help you create and customize WordPress plugins and templates. Think of it as a hands-on guide with all the essential steps simplified, leaving the heavy lifting to AI so you can focus on making your ideas shine.

Here's a sneak peek of what we'll cover together:

Embrace Your Inner "Idiot"

Let's shatter the myth that you need deep technical knowledge to create something impactful. In this chapter, you'll learn how a beginner's mindset can actually be a massive advantage and how AI can help you bridge the gap between your ideas and their execution.

Getting Started with AI Tools

You'll meet the essential AI tools that will change your approach to WordPress development. From ChatGPT, which can generate code snippets and answer questions, to must-have plugins that streamline your workflow, this chapter sets you up for success.

Step-by-Step Plugin Development
Here's where the magic happens! I'll walk you through creating your very first WordPress plugin. From concept to functionality, you'll learn how to brainstorm, code, and troubleshoot with the help of AI, making plugin development accessible and fun.

Designing Your First Template
This chapter is all about aesthetics. We'll explore WordPress templates and show you how to create a design that reflects your vision without requiring a deep dive into complex code.

Automation Made Simple
Discover how to make your site more efficient with automation tools like Zapier. By automating repetitive tasks, you'll enhance your website's performance and save time, making your site work harder for you.

Testing, Troubleshooting, and Optimization
We'll take the guesswork out of testing and optimizing your site. Here, you'll learn how AI can help you identify bugs, suggest solutions, and fine-tune your site's speed and user experience.

Easy Deployment (with my secret tools!)
In this final chapter, we'll go live! I'll show you how to package and deploy your plugin or template with simple steps and a few secret tools, exclusively revealed in a video guide. You'll finish with a product you're ready to launch into the world.

Common Challenges and Practical Solutions
Creating something new isn't always straightforward—it's a journey of trial, error, and discovery. If you're facing code anxiety, confusing jargon, or technical roadblocks, you're not alone. In this book, I'll share practical solutions for overcoming common challenges, like unfamiliar terminology, troubleshooting tips, and strategies to stay motivated even when you hit a snag. AI will be there to support you along the way, stepping in to clarify, correct, and guide.

Let's Make an Impact, Together
1% Developer, 99% Idiot! is more than a book; it's an invitation to create, to experiment, and to discover what's possible. By the time you reach the final page, you'll be ready to create for yourself, launch a business, or even build solutions for others. Whether you're looking to add functionality to a site, create a unique template, or explore the future of AI-powered development, this book equips you with the tools and the confidence to make it happen.

So, grab your laptop, set aside any doubts, and let's get started. The only thing you truly need is your creativity; AI will handle the rest. Ready to become a WordPress wizard? Let's dive in and let 1% Developer, 99% Idiot! show you just how fun and achievable building your ideas can be.

Chapter 1: Embrace Your Inner "Idiot"

Welcome to the start of your journey! We're going to kick things off by embracing a surprising idea: not knowing everything is actually a superpower. I know, it might sound strange, but here's the truth—feeling like a "beginner" or even an "idiot" isn't a disadvantage; it's an asset.

When you're new to something, you're free from preconceived notions, which lets you experiment without the pressure of getting it "right" on the first try. In tech, we call this approach the beginner's mindset—a mindset that allows you to be curious, creative, and bold enough to make mistakes and learn from them.

In this chapter, I'll show you why you don't need to be a coding expert to start building. With a beginner's mindset and the help of AI tools, creating a WordPress plugin or template is more achievable than you might think. So, let's embrace that inner "idiot," let go of any fears of not knowing everything, and get ready to explore!

Advantages of a Beginner's Mindset

The beginner's mindset is more than just starting fresh; it's a powerful tool for innovation and creativity. Here's why:

Fresh Perspective

When you're new to something, you're not weighed down by the "rules" and limitations that experienced developers might feel. You can think outside the box, ask what might seem like "silly" questions, and find solutions that are simple but effective. This openness often leads to creative breakthroughs.

Freedom to Experiment

Experts can get stuck following conventional methods. Beginners, on the other hand, have the freedom to experiment. Since you're not burdened by industry "standards" yet, you can focus on creating and learning without being too hard on yourself.

Curiosity and Resilience

Starting something new means there will be a learning curve. But as a beginner, you're driven by curiosity, and that curiosity builds resilience. Every expert was once a beginner who learned by trying, failing, and trying again.

These qualities make the beginner's mindset a huge advantage in tech. Remember, the goal isn't perfection; it's to make progress. With AI's help, you'll see that progress come faster than you might expect.

How AI Bridges the Gap Between Ideas and Technical Execution

Now, let's talk about the real game-changer: AI. Think of it as your personal tech assistant, ready to help whenever you're unsure. Tools like ChatGPT act as translators between your ideas and the technical skills needed to make them happen.

AI as Your Personal Coding Assistant

AI can help in countless ways, from generating code snippets to explaining complex concepts step-by-step. Imagine having an experienced developer available 24/7 to guide you through each task—that's AI for you. Here's how you can start using AI as your coding assistant:

Generate Simple Code Snippets: Instead of struggling to write code from scratch, you can ask AI to generate the basics for you. Try prompting ChatGPT with something like "Generate a WordPress code snippet that displays 'Hello, World!' on the homepage." The AI handles the technical part, so you can focus on what the code should do.

Understand Code Line-by-Line: When you come across a piece of code that looks confusing, just ask AI to break it down. For example, prompt it with "Explain this code line-by-line," and you'll get a clear, beginner-friendly explanation.

By using AI to bridge the gap, you're not just cutting down on the technical intimidation—you're also bringing your ideas to life, one prompt at a time. With

AI as your assistant, it's okay to dive in without fully understanding everything; the tools are here to guide you.

Practical Exercises

Let's turn these ideas into action. The following exercises will help you start brainstorming plugin ideas and experimenting with AI to see real results.

Exercise 1: Brainstorm Plugin Ideas

Goal: Inspire creativity and get you thinking about useful WordPress plugins.
Instructions: Set aside 10 minutes to brainstorm ideas for WordPress plugins. Think about things you'd like your website to do or features that might be useful. Here are a few examples to get you started:

A daily motivational quote generator for your homepage.
A welcome message that changes depending on the time of day.
A "contact me" popup with customizable prompts.

Write down at least three ideas. Don't worry about whether they're "possible" right now—just let your creativity flow.
Review your ideas and choose one that excites you. We'll be building on this idea in later chapters, so pick something you're interested in.
Outcome:
By writing down your ideas, you'll start to focus on what you want to build, and you'll see that the possibilities are endless, even without extensive technical knowledge.

Exercise 2: Testing AI for Code Generation
Goal:
Introduce you to using AI as a coding assistant and see the power of AI-generated code firsthand.

Instructions:
Open ChatGPT or any AI-powered code generator you have access to.
Try entering a simple prompt like: "Generate a WordPress plugin that displays a welcome message."

Copy the generated code and paste it into the functions.php file of a WordPress theme (we'll cover how to set up your environment in the next chapter).
Visit your site to see the result! If you want to change the message, try adjusting your prompt and testing again.

Outcome:
You'll gain hands-on experience with AI-generated code, learning how to prompt AI for changes and see real results on your WordPress site.

Summary & Key Takeaways

- Let's recap what we've covered in this chapter:

Embrace the beginner's mindset: A fresh perspective, the freedom to experiment, and curiosity are powerful tools that help you learn and create.
AI is your coding partner: Tools like ChatGPT act as assistants that bridge the gap between your ideas and the technical skills required to bring them to life.
Experimentation is key: Don't worry about understanding everything perfectly right now. Try things out, play with code, and remember—AI is here to guide you through the process.

Chapter 2:
Getting Started with AI Tools

Let's dive into the world of AI-enhanced development! This chapter is all about getting set up with the tools that will make plugin creation intuitive and fast, allowing you to experiment safely within a local WordPress environment. Here, I'll guide you step-by-step to set up essential tools, work with an AI-driven development environment, and start using the power of artificial intelligence to make coding as smooth as possible.

1. Understanding Your AI Tools: ChatGPT and Cursor

Before we jump in, let's clarify what each tool does and how you'll be using them throughout this book.

ChatGPT:

Think of ChatGPT as your coding consultant. This conversational AI can generate code snippets, troubleshoot issues, and explain technical concepts in plain language. It's available directly in a browser and works with prompts, meaning you simply type in what you need, and ChatGPT will respond. Throughout this book, I'll provide specific prompts you can use to make ChatGPT work efficiently for you.

Cursor:

Cursor is a powerful code editor with AI integration, making it the perfect tool for real-time coding assistance. This app is ideal for Mac users, supporting multiple OSs and environments, and it's equipped with intelligent code suggestions and editing features. Cursor will help you code faster, allowing you to see and test results directly in your development environment without switching between tools.

Example Setup with AI Tools:

Imagine you want to create a plugin that displays a customized welcome message based on the user's location. Using ChatGPT, you can prompt it with something like:

"Write a WordPress plugin that displays a custom welcome message based on the user's country."

ChatGPT will generate the initial code, which you can then paste into Cursor to edit and refine further. As you make changes, Cursor's AI will suggest improvements and corrections in real time, making the entire process smooth and interactive.

2. Setting Up Your Local WordPress Environment with Local by Flywheel

To build, test, and refine your plugins safely, you'll need a local environment—a private, isolated WordPress installation that runs on your computer. Local by Flywheel is a top-notch tool for this purpose, offering a user-friendly setup and seamless integration with WordPress. Let's set it up step-by-step.

Step-by-Step Guide: Setting Up Local by Flywheel
Download and Install Local by Flywheel:
Visit and download the application.
Install it by following the on-screen instructions. This will create an environment where WordPress runs on your computer without affecting any live websites.

Create a New WordPress Site in Local:
Open Local by Flywheel and click "Create a New Site."
Name your site something like "My Plugin Sandbox," select preferred options for environment settings (the default PHP and MySQL versions are fine), and finalize the setup.
Once the setup is complete, open the site in your browser using Local's one-click access.

Explore Your Local WordPress Site:
Log in to your new WordPress site at localhost/your-site-name/wp-admin. Spend a few minutes exploring the dashboard and settings. This local site will be your playground for testing plugins and experimenting with code.

Optional - Enable Developer Tools in Local:
Go to the "**Tools**" tab in Local to enable additional developer features, such as PHPMyAdmin for database access or Mailhog for testing email functionality.
Pro Tip: Bookmark this local WordPress login page for quick access. You'll be returning to this site frequently as we test and develop plugins.

3. Practical Exercise: Generating and Testing Code Snippets with AI

Now that your environment is set up, let's dive into a practical exercise to generate a simple WordPress plugin using AI, then test it in your local environment.

Exercise: Create a Custom Welcome Message Plugin
Objective: Create a basic WordPress plugin that displays a custom welcome message on your site's homepage.
Instructions:
Open ChatGPT:
In your browser, open ChatGPT and get ready to enter a prompt.
Prompt ChatGPT for Code:

Enter the following prompt:
"Generate a WordPress plugin that displays a custom welcome message on the homepage. Allow the message to be easily customizable from the admin dashboard."
Review and Copy the Code:

ChatGPT will provide code, typically structured with a PHP file that defines the plugin and a function that outputs the welcome message.

Copy the code provided by ChatGPT.

Paste the Code in Cursor:

Open the Cursor app, create a new file named custom-welcome-plugin.php, and paste the code.

Save this file to the wp-content/plugins directory in your Local site's folder (you can find it under Local's settings > "Open site folder").

Activate the Plugin in WordPress:

Go to your WordPress dashboard, navigate to Plugins > Installed Plugins, and activate the "Custom Welcome Message" plugin.

Visit your site's homepage to check if the welcome message is displayed. You should see a message that can be customized from the admin area.

Experiment with Customization:

In the WordPress dashboard, go to Settings > Custom Welcome Message (or similar, depending on the plugin structure). Customize the message text, save the changes, and refresh the homepage to see your updates.

Outcome:

You've created, customized, and tested your first AI-generated plugin! This exercise gives you hands-on experience with AI-assisted code generation, as well as the practical steps to implement and modify a WordPress plugin on a local environment.

4. Exploring Additional AI Prompts and Modifications

Now that you've created a basic plugin, let's look at a few additional prompts to enhance your plugin with AI assistance.
Advanced Prompts to Try with ChatGPT:
Adding Conditional Logic:
Prompt: "Modify the welcome message plugin to display different messages based on the time of day (morning, afternoon, evening)."
Test: See if ChatGPT adds conditional logic in PHP to adjust the message based on server time.
Styling the Message with CSS:
Prompt: "Add inline CSS to the welcome message so it displays with a blue background, white text, and padding."
Test: Place the updated code in Cursor and reload your site to see the styled message.
Creating a Shortcode for the Welcome Message:
Prompt: "Rewrite the plugin to use a shortcode for displaying the welcome message anywhere on the site."
Test: Use [welcome_message] (or similar shortcode generated by ChatGPT) in a page or post to display the welcome message wherever you like.
Each of these prompts demonstrates how versatile AI-generated code can be, allowing you to expand functionality and customize your plugin to suit specific needs.

5. Troubleshooting Tips for AI-Generated Code

As you experiment with AI-generated code, you may run into common issues. Here are a few examples and tips on how to resolve them:
Issue: The code doesn't execute as expected.
Solution: Double-check that you pasted the code in the right file (custom-welcome-plugin.php) and activated the plugin in WordPress. If you receive

errors, try asking ChatGPT to troubleshoot with a prompt like, "What could cause a welcome message plugin to not display on WordPress?"

Issue: Code suggestions from AI are outdated or incompatible.

Solution: Update your prompt to specify the WordPress version, like "Generate a WordPress 6.0-compatible plugin for displaying a welcome message."

Issue: Styling or layout doesn't appear as intended.

Solution: Try prompting ChatGPT with detailed styling instructions, or ask for help in debugging by providing context, e.g., "My welcome message plugin isn't displaying the CSS correctly. Can you suggest improvements?"

6.
Summary & Key Takeaways

Here's a quick recap of what we've covered in this chapter:

AI tools are your partners: ChatGPT and Cursor are your main allies, generating code snippets, assisting with edits, and enhancing your understanding of complex concepts.

A local WordPress environment is essential: Local by Flywheel provides a safe space for experimentation, allowing you to test your plugins before deploying them to a live site.

Hands-on practice is key: With each exercise, you gain confidence and refine your skills, preparing you for more complex plugin development in upcoming chapters.

With your setup complete and your first plugin tested, you're ready to go deeper. In Chapter 3: Building Your First Plugin, we'll walk through the creation of a more complex plugin, refining your skills in development and customization. Ready to dive in? Let's build something amazing!

Chapter 3: Building Your First Plugin

Objective:
Create a simple but functional WordPress plugin that greets visitors based on the time of day. This chapter will walk you through setting up the plugin's structure, adding functionality, and using AI tools for assistance, code generation, and troubleshooting.

1. Understanding Plugin Basics

Before we dive in, let's go over what makes up a WordPress plugin. A plugin is essentially a collection of PHP files that add specific functionality to WordPress sites without changing the core code. Plugins are modular, so you can activate or deactivate them easily from the WordPress dashboard.

Each plugin typically consists of:

Header	Functions	Hooks and Shortcodes
Declares the plugin name, description, version, and author.	These are the actions the plugin performs.	These control where and how the plugin integrates with WordPress.

In this chapter, we'll create a plugin that displays a greeting message based on the time of day. Let's get started!

2. Setting Up the Plugin Structure

Step 1: Create the Plugin Folder and File
In your WordPress site's wp-content/plugins directory, create a new folder named greeting-plugin.
Inside this folder, create a PHP file named greeting-plugin.php.

Step 2: Add the Plugin Header
Open greeting-plugin.php and start by adding the plugin header:

```php
*/
Plugin Name: Greeting Plugin
Description: Displays a greeting message based on the time of day.
Version: 1.0
Author: João Castro
*/
```

Explanation: The header provides essential information to WordPress so it can identify and display the plugin in the dashboard. This is the minimal setup needed for WordPress to recognize the plugin.

Step 3: Enqueue Styles and Scripts (Optional)
If you want to style the greeting message or add interactive JavaScript, you can enqueue CSS and JavaScript files here. However, for this simple plugin, we'll stick with basic PHP.

3. Creating the Greeting Function

Now that our plugin is set up, let's add the main functionality: a greeting message that changes based on the time of day.

Step 1: Define the Greeting Function
In greeting-plugin.php, add the following code below the header:

```php
$hour = date("H");

if ($hour < 12) {
    $greeting = "Good morning!";
} elseif ($hour < 18) {
    $greeting = "Good afternoon!";
} else {
    $greeting = "Good evening!";
}

return "<div class='greeting-message'>$greeting Welcome to our site!</div>";
}
```

Explanation: This function checks the current hour using PHP's date() function. Depending on the hour, it sets the greeting to "Good morning," "Good afternoon," or "Good evening."

Step 2: Add a Shortcode
To allow users to place the greeting anywhere on their site, we'll create a shortcode.

Add the following code after the greeting function:

```php
add_shortcode('greeting_message',
'gp_display_greeting');
}
add_action('init', 'gp_register_greeting_shortcode');
```

Explanation: The add_shortcode() function registers the [greeting_message] shortcode, which can be placed anywhere on the site to display the greeting.

Step 3: Style the Greeting Message (Optional)

If you'd like, add a bit of CSS to style the greeting message. Create a greeting-plugin.css file in the greeting-plugin folder and add some basic styles:

```css
.greeting-message {
    font-size: 24px;
    font-weight: bold;
    text-align: center;
    margin-top: 20px;
}
```

To load this CSS file, add the following code to greeting-plugin.php:

```
wp_enqueue_style('gp-greeting-style',
plugin_dir_url(__FILE__) . 'greeting-plugin.css');
}
add_action('wp_enqueue_scripts', 'gp_enqueue_styles');
```

Explanation: This function loads the CSS file, giving the greeting message a simple style.

4. Testing the Plugin with AI Assistance

Now that we have our plugin set up, let's test it out!
Activate the Plugin: Go to **Plugins > Installed Plugins** in your WordPress dashboard and activate the "**Greeting Plugin.**"
Add the Shortcode: Create a new page or post, and add the [greeting_message] shortcode.
View the Result: Visit the page to see your greeting message displayed with the correct greeting based on the time of day.

5. Using AI to Customize the Plugin

Now that you've got the basic plugin working, let's use AI to make some enhancements. Here are a few ways you can modify the plugin with AI prompts.
Customization 1: Adding User Location to the Greeting
Use ChatGPT to personalize the greeting by adding the visitor's city using a geolocation API.
Prompt:
"Modify the Greeting Plugin to include the visitor's city in the greeting. Use a geolocation API to detect the city based on the user's IP address."

Expected Outcome:
ChatGPT will add code to integrate with a geolocation API (like IPinfo or Geoplugin) to detect and display the user's city, resulting in a more personalized greeting.

Customization 2: Creating a Settings Page for the Plugin

You can add options in the WordPress admin to customize the greeting message directly from the dashboard.

Prompt:
"Add a settings page to the Greeting Plugin that allows the site admin to customize the morning, afternoon, and evening messages."

Expected Outcome:
ChatGPT will generate code to create a settings page in the WordPress admin, where users can enter custom messages for each time period. This lets site owners personalize the experience further without editing code.

Customization 3: Add an Optional Background Color
Use CSS to add a custom background color option for the greeting message.

Prompt:
"Modify the Greeting Plugin to include an optional background color for the greeting message, with options to choose the color from the settings page."

Expected Outcome:
This customization allows site admins to set a background color through the settings page. ChatGPT will provide CSS and PHP code to enable color customization.

6.
Troubleshooting Common Issues with AI

As you work with the plugin, you may encounter some common issues. Here's how you can resolve them with AI:

Issue: The greeting doesn't display.
Solution: Double-check that the shortcode [greeting_message] is placed on the page. If it still doesn't work, prompt ChatGPT with, "Troubleshoot why my shortcode isn't displaying in my WordPress plugin."

Issue: Customizations aren't appearing.

Solution: Make sure to refresh the page after saving changes in the settings. If styles or settings don't update, you can ask ChatGPT, "Why aren't my plugin settings updating?" for insights.

Issue: Error messages in WordPress.

Solution: Paste the error into ChatGPT for suggestions. Prompt: "How do I fix this error in my WordPress plugin?" ChatGPT can provide explanations and possible solutions for specific error messages.

7. Summary & Key Takeaways

Here's a recap of what we accomplished in this chapter:

Built a simple, functional plugin: You created a WordPress plugin that displays a time-based greeting message.

Enhanced the plugin using AI: With ChatGPT, you explored ways to expand functionality by adding user location, customizable settings, and background options.

Troubleshot issues with AI assistance: You learned to resolve common plugin issues with the help of AI, making development smoother.

This chapter has given you a solid foundation in creating WordPress plugins, using AI to make development easier and more flexible. In the next chapter, Chapter 4: Designing Your First Template, we'll apply the same principles to design, customizing templates without getting lost in code.

Let's continue building and learning!

Chapter 4: Designing Your First Template

Objective:
Create a custom WordPress template that aligns with your vision for site aesthetics, using AI to help streamline the design process. This chapter will guide you through building a basic WordPress template and enhancing it with AI-assisted customizations, from layout structure to CSS styling.

1. Understanding Templates in WordPress

In WordPress, a template controls the layout and design of individual pages, posts, or specific parts of your website, such as headers and footers. Templates allow you to customize how content is displayed and organized, without altering the underlying data.

Key template files you'll encounter:

header.php: Controls the header section (e.g., logo, navigation).

footer.php: Defines the footer section.

single.php: Used for individual posts.

page.php: Defines how pages are displayed.

In this chapter, we'll start by creating a simple custom page template, then use AI to add styling and layout elements that bring it to life.

2. Setting Up Your Custom Template

To create a custom template, we'll work within your active theme's directory.

Step 1: Create the Template File

Access Your Theme's Directory: Open wp-content/themes/your-active-theme.

Create a New PHP File:

In this folder, create a file named custom-template.php.

Add the Template Header: Open the file and start with the following header code, which tells WordPress that this is a template file:

```php
<?php
/*
Template Name: Custom Greeting Page
Description: A custom page template with a personalized greeting.
*/
?>
```

Explanation: The header allows WordPress to recognize this as a selectable template in the page editor.

Step 2: Add Basic Template Structure

Add basic HTML and PHP code to structure the page:

```php
get_header(); // Includes the header
?>

<div class="content-container">
    <h1>Welcome to Your Custom Greeting Page</h1>
    <p><?php echo do_shortcode('[greeting_message]'); ?></p>
</div>

get_footer(); // Includes the footer
?>
```

Explanation: This template includes the standard header and footer and uses the [greeting_message] shortcode to display a greeting message. The container has a simple heading and paragraph for the greeting text.

3. Styling the Template with AI Assistance

Now that we have a basic structure, let's add some custom styling. Here's where AI can help generate the CSS for the design. Prompt for CSS Styling with AI to add visual flair, ask ChatGPT for a basic CSS style for your template's container.

Here's a sample prompt:

> "Generate CSS for a content container with a background color, rounded corners, padding, and centered text that would work well on a WordPress custom page template."

Response from ChatGPT (Example CSS):

```css
.content-container {
   background-color: #f9f9f9;
   border-radius: 10px;
   padding: 20px;
   max-width: 800px;
   margin: 20px auto;
   text-align: center;
   box-shadow: 0px 4px 8px rgba(0, 0, 0, 0.1);
   font-family: Arial, sans-serif;
}
```

Adding the CSS to Your Theme

In your theme's folder, open the style.css file or create a custom CSS file if preferred.

Paste the generated CSS code into this file.

Save the changes and refresh the page to see the new styles.

Result: The greeting message should now appear in a styled container, centered and visually distinct, with a subtle shadow effect.

4. Using AI to Add Dynamic Elements

Let's add a few more advanced elements to the template with AI assistance, such as a background image or conditional greetings based on the visitor's location.

Adding a Background Image with AI

You can use AI to help you set up dynamic background images that change based on conditions, such as time of day.

Prompt for Dynamic Background:

> "Modify the CSS to use a different background image for morning, afternoon, and evening on a WordPress page template. Generate CSS with media queries or JavaScript as needed."

AI-Generated Solution (Example Code):

```css
body.custom-template-morning .content-container {
    background-image: url('path/to/morning-image.jpg');
}

body.custom-template-afternoon .content-container {
    background-image: url('path/to/afternoon-image.jpg');
}

body.custom-template-evening .content-container {
    background-image: url('path/to/evening-image.jpg');
}
```

JavaScript to Add Classes Based on Time:

```js
body.custom-template-morning .content-container {
document.addEventListener("DOMContentLoaded", function()
{
    const hour = new Date().getHours();
    let timeClass = "";

    if (hour < 12) {
       timeClass = "custom-template-morning";
    } else if (hour < 18) {
       timeClass = "custom-template-afternoon";
    } else {
       timeClass = "custom-template-evening";
    }

    document.body.classList.add(timeClass);
});
```

Add CSS to style.css: Include the CSS generated by ChatGPT for background images in your theme's style.css.

Include JavaScript: Save the JavaScript in a file named template-time.js in your theme folder. Enqueue it in functions.php:

```
function custom_template_scripts() {
    wp_enqueue_script('template-time-script',
get_template_directory_uri() . '/template-time.js',
array(), null, true);
}
add_action('wp_enqueue_scripts',
'custom_template_scripts');
```

The template's background will now change based on the time of day.

5. Adding Custom Template Options in the WordPress Admin

Let's add a customization option in the WordPress admin for site owners to change the greeting message text directly.

Step 1: Register a Settings Field
In functions.php, add the following code to create a settings field:

```
    register_setting('general', 'greeting_text');
    add_settings_field(
        'greeting_text',
        'Custom Greeting Text',
        'greeting_text_callback',
        'general'
    );
}
add_action('admin_init', 'custom_template_settings_init');

    $greeting_text = get_option('greeting_text', 'Welcome!');
    echo "<input type='text' id='greeting_text' name='greeting_text' value='" . esc_attr($greeting_text) . "' />";
}
```

Explanation: This code adds a field under **Settings > General** in WordPress for customizing the greeting text.

Step 2: Update the Template to Display Custom Greeting
In custom-template.php, replace the greeting text with the saved admin option:

```
$greeting_text = get_option('greeting_text',
'Welcome!');
echo "<p>$greeting_text</p>";
```

Site owners can now set a custom greeting text from the WordPress admin.

6. Testing and Troubleshooting with AI

As you add more dynamic features, it's essential to test the template thoroughly. Use AI to help troubleshoot if you encounter issues.

Common Issues
Background not displaying correctly: Double-check the CSS and file paths.

Prompt ChatGPT with:

> "Troubleshoot background image not loading on my WordPress template."

Settings not saving: Ensure the register_setting and add_settings_field functions are correctly set up. Prompt ChatGPT with "Why is my custom WordPress setting not saving?"

7. Summary & Key Takeaways

Here's a recap of what we accomplished in this chapter:

Created a custom template: You built a basic custom page template that uses WordPress shortcodes.

Styled and enhanced the template using AI: With ChatGPT's help, you added CSS for styling and JavaScript for dynamic background images.

Added customization options in the WordPress admin: You created a settings field to allow site admins to edit the greeting text without touching code.

With a custom template created and customized, you're ready for the next chapter, where we'll explore Automation Made Simple. You'll learn how to make your site more efficient by automating tasks like content updates, saving time and keeping your site fresh.

Let's keep building and learning!

Chapter 5: Automation Made Simple

Objective:
Learn how to automate key tasks on your WordPress site using AI and automation tools. This chapter will focus on setting up automated processes that save time, enhance user experience, and ensure a more dynamic, engaging website. From automating content updates to implementing scheduled messages and user notifications, you'll explore powerful automation techniques to streamline your site.

1. Why Automate Your WordPress Site?

Automation simplifies repetitive tasks and frees up your time for more important work, like creating content or engaging with users. With AI and tools like Zapier and IFTTT (If This Then That), you can automate various aspects of your WordPress site. This chapter will guide you through automating:

Content updates: Automatically publish scheduled updates, seasonal messages, or daily posts.

Notifications: Set up alerts and notifications to keep users engaged.

Integrations: Connect WordPress with other platforms, such as social media, for automatic cross-posting.

Let's start by exploring the tools and methods that make automation easy and effective.

2. Choosing the Right Automation Tools

To begin automating tasks on your WordPress site, you'll need to choose tools that align with your needs. Here are two powerful options for WordPress automation:

Zapier: Zapier connects WordPress with thousands of apps and automates workflows called "Zaps." Each Zap is a "trigger-action" sequence; for example, when you publish a post on WordPress, Zapier can automatically share it on social media.

IFTTT: Similar to Zapier, IFTTT uses "applets" to create automation sequences. For example, you can set an applet to send a notification to your phone every time a new comment is posted on your WordPress site.
Both tools work with a wide range of applications and offer free plans for basic usage, making them excellent for beginners.

3. Automating Content Updates

Content is key to engaging users, but updating it regularly can be time-consuming. Let's use automation to publish scheduled updates and seasonal messages.

Example: Schedule Automated Seasonal Greetings
Suppose you want your site to display special greetings for specific holidays or seasons automatically. We'll use a plugin for this task, combined with AI-generated messages.

Step 1: Install and Configure the WP Scheduled Posts Plugin

Go to **Plugins** > **Add New** in your WordPress dashboard.
Search for WP Scheduled Posts and install the plugin.
Once activated, go to the plugin's settings to schedule posts and updates in advance.

Step 2: Use ChatGPT to Generate Seasonal Greetings
Prompt ChatGPT for festive or seasonal greetings that fit various holidays.

Here's a sample prompt:

> "Generate a list of short seasonal greetings for New Year, Easter, Halloween, and Christmas that I can schedule to display on my WordPress site."

Example Response from ChatGPT:

- New Year: "Happy New Year! May this year bring you joy, success, and inspiration."

- Easter: "Wishing you a joyful Easter filled with peace and renewal."

- Halloween: "Happy Halloween! May your day be filled with treats and no tricks!"

- Christmas: "Merry Christmas! Wishing you warmth, joy, and family fun."

Step 3: Schedule Greetings for Each Season

With WP Scheduled Posts, create individual posts or page updates with your seasonal greetings and schedule them for the relevant dates. This way, your site will automatically update with timely greetings without requiring any manual input.

4. Automating Notifications for User Engagement

Notifications help you keep users engaged, especially when they are timely and relevant. Let's set up automatic notifications for new content and important updates.

Example: Send Email Notifications for New Blog Posts

To notify subscribers automatically when new content is published, you can use the MailPoet plugin, which integrates well with WordPress for email automation.

Step 1: Install and Configure MailPoet

Go to **Plugins** > **Add New** and search for MailPoet.

Install and activate the plugin.

Set up a mailing list in MailPoet and design an email template that will be sent out whenever a new post is published.

Step 2: Use ChatGPT to Customize the Notification Message

Prompt ChatGPT to help you write an engaging notification email.

> "Write a short, friendly email notification that invites subscribers to check out our latest blog post."

Example Response from ChatGPT:

> Subject: New Post Alert! Check Out Our Latest Update
>
> Message:
> Hey [Subscriber Name]!
>
> We just published something new on [Blog Name] that we think you'll love. Head over to the site to check it out, and let us know what you think! We're always excited to hear from you.
>
> Happy reading!
> [Your Blog Name] Team

This email can be added to MailPoet's automation sequence, so each new post automatically triggers a friendly notification to your subscribers.

5. Automating Social Media Sharing

Keeping social media updated can be a hassle. Fortunately, you can automate this process using Zapier to connect WordPress with platforms like Twitter, Facebook, or LinkedIn.

Example: Share New Posts on Social Media Automatically
Here's how to set up a Zap that shares new WordPress posts on Twitter:
Sign Up for Zapier: If you don't have an account, sign up for free at.

Create a New Zap:
Trigger: Choose WordPress as the app, select "New Post" as the trigger.
Action: Select Twitter (or another social media platform) as the app, and choose "Create Tweet" as the action.

Customize the Tweet: Use a template such as "Check out our latest post: {{PostTitle}} - {{PostURL}}" to include the title and link of the new post.

Test and Activate the Zap: Zapier will test the connection, and if successful, activate it. Now, each new post will automatically be shared on Twitter.

Pro Tip: Customize messages for each platform using variations generated by ChatGPT to ensure your social media posts are engaging and varied.

6. Using AI to Enhance Automation

AI can play a key role in enhancing automation by generating dynamic, customized content for each automation type. Here are a few additional AI-driven automations to try:

AI-Powered Daily Content Ideas

Automate content planning by generating new ideas every day.

Prompt for Daily Content Ideas:

> "Provide a unique daily topic idea for a blog post on [Your Niche] to help me plan content for my WordPress blog."

ChatGPT can generate new ideas, which you can then store in a spreadsheet or calendar tool like Google Calendar to keep your content pipeline filled.

Automatically Generate "Did You Know?" Facts for a Widget

Display a new "Did You Know?" fact every day using a simple plugin and ChatGPT for fact generation.

> "Provide 30 interesting 'Did You Know?' facts about [Your Niche] that I can use for my WordPress site."

Upload these facts to a plugin or widget that cycles through daily updates, ensuring fresh content every day.

7. Advanced Automation with IFTTT

IFTTT can automate even more specific tasks, such as sending a text message when certain conditions are met on your WordPress site.
Example: Receive a Text Notification for New Comments
Set up an applet in IFTTT that sends you a text message every time a new comment is posted on your WordPress site.
Create an IFTTT Account: Go to and create an account.
Create a New Applet:
Trigger: Select WordPress and choose "New Comment."
Action: Choose "Send Notification" or "Send SMS" to receive a message directly on your phone.
Customize the Message: Create a custom message like, "New comment on [Post Title]: [CommentContent]".
Result: This way, you'll stay updated in real-time and can quickly engage with commenters on your site.

8. Troubleshooting and Testing Your Automations

After setting up automation, it's essential to test each workflow to ensure it works correctly. Here are some troubleshooting tips:
Emails not sending: Ensure the MailPoet plugin is correctly configured with your mailing list and that your email server settings are up-to-date.
Social media posts not appearing: Verify that the Zap in Zapier is active and test it by publishing a test post on your WordPress site.
Scheduled posts not updating: Double-check the schedule and ensure your time zone is set correctly in WordPress.

If issues arise, use ChatGPT to guide you with troubleshooting prompts such as "Why are my MailPoet emails not sending?" or "What could cause scheduled WordPress posts to fail?"

9. Summary & Key Takeaways

Here's what we accomplished in this chapter:

- **Automated content updates:** Scheduled posts and seasonal greetings allow you to keep content fresh without constant manual updates.
- **Set up user notifications**: Automated emails and SMS notifications keep users and admins engaged and informed.
- Used AI to customize automations: AI-generated content for emails, social posts, and "Did You Know?" facts adds a dynamic touch to automation.
- Integrated social media automation: You set up workflows to share posts on social media automatically.

Automation simplifies WordPress management, making it more efficient, engaging, and responsive. In the next chapter, Chapter 6: Testing, Troubleshooting, and Optimization, we'll explore methods to test, troubleshoot, and optimize your site's performance, ensuring a smooth, user-friendly experience.

Let's continue our journey to a fully functional, efficient, and creative WordPress site!

Chapter 6: Testing, Troubleshooting, Optimization, and Security

Objective:
Ensure your WordPress site is secure, optimized, and functioning smoothly. This chapter covers testing and troubleshooting techniques, AI-driven performance optimization, and essential security practices to protect your plugins, templates, and site as a whole.

1. The Role of AI in Testing, Optimization and Security

AI can be a powerful ally in identifying issues, improving performance, and securing your site. From debugging plugins to implementing targeted optimizations, AI helps you stay on top of site performance and security. In this chapter, we'll use AI to:

Test and troubleshoot plugin and template functionality.
Improve performance metrics.
Integrate essential security practices into your WordPress site and plugins.

2. Testing Your Site's Functionality and Security

Testing is crucial to ensure that your plugins, templates, and automations work correctly and don't introduce security vulnerabilities. Here's how to conduct a thorough local test of your work.

Step 1: Test Plugin and Template Functionality
In your local environment (as set up in Chapter 2), verify the performance of each feature:

Plugin Shortcodes and Widgets: Add and verify all shortcodes and widgets for correct display and interaction.
Forms and Inputs: Test any forms, inputs, or fields to ensure they behave as expected.
User Role Permissions: Confirm that only authorized user roles have access to plugin settings or admin features to maintain secure access control.

Step 2: Security Testing Using AI
AI tools like ChatGPT can help identify potential security issues in your code, including vulnerabilities in form handling, database queries, and input sanitization.

Prompt for Security Review:

> "Review this WordPress plugin code for common security vulnerabilities like SQL injection, XSS, and file inclusion vulnerabilities."

Expected AI Review: ChatGPT will review your code, identify potential vulnerabilities, and suggest security measures, such as sanitizing inputs, escaping outputs, and using WordPress's nonce validation for form submissions.

Step 3: Use AI to Generate Secure Code Enhancements

For enhanced security, use AI to generate code snippets that follow secure practices, like input sanitization and escaping outputs.

Example Prompt for Input Sanitization:

"Generate PHP code that sanitizes input fields and escapes output for a WordPress form submission."

```
function sanitize_form_input($data) {
    return sanitize_text_field($data);
}
    echo esc_html($data);
}
```

This sanitization and escaping prevent SQL injections, cross-site scripting (XSS), and other common attacks.

3. Optimizing Site Performance with GTmetrix and AI

Performance is key for both user experience and SEO. GTmetrix provides detailed insights into site speed, which you can address with AI-driven code improvements.

Step 1: Run a GTmetrix Test
Go to and run a performance test.

Review the performance scores, including Largest Contentful Paint (LCP) and Total Blocking Time (TBT). GTmetrix will highlight specific optimization opportunities, such as reducing image sizes or minimizing CSS and JavaScript.

Step 2: Use AI to Generate Performance Improvements
AI can generate specific code-based solutions for issues flagged by GTmetrix. Here are common optimization strategies you can implement with AI assistance.

Example 1: Minifying JavaScript and CSS
Reducing file sizes by minifying CSS and JavaScript can significantly improve load times.

Prompt for ChatGPT:

> "Generate PHP code for a WordPress plugin that minifies JavaScript and CSS files to improve site performance."

Expected Code:

```
function my_minify_assets() {
    wp_enqueue_script('main-js', get_template_directory_uri() . '/js/main.js', array(), null, true);
    wp_add_inline_script('main-js', 'document.addEventListener("DOMContentLoaded", function(){/* Minified JS here */});');

    wp_enqueue_style('main-css', get_template_directory_uri() . '/css/style.css', array(), null, 'all');
    wp_add_inline_style('main-css', '/* Minified CSS here */');
}
add_action('wp_enqueue_scripts', 'my_minify_assets');
```

Example 2: Lazy Loading Images with AI

Lazy loading delays loading of images until they are in view, reducing initial load time.

Prompt for ChatGPT:

> "Generate code for a WordPress plugin that implements lazy loading for images on all pages."

Expected Code:

```
document.addEventListener("DOMContentLoaded", function() {
    const images = document.querySelectorAll("img");
    images.forEach(img => {
        img.setAttribute("loading", "lazy");
    });
});
```

This JavaScript snippet can be added to a custom plugin or theme, reducing image load times and optimizing the site.

4. Securing Your Site Against Common Vulnerabilities

Given your experience in ethical hacking, integrating robust security practices is essential. Here are the main security areas to address with AI-assisted solutions.

Example 1: Nonce Verification for Secure Form Handling
Nonces prevent cross-site request forgery (CSRF) attacks by verifying form requests.

Prompt for ChatGPT:

"Generate WordPress code to add nonce verification to a form submission for enhanced security."

Expected Code:

```
function secure_form_nonce_field() {
    wp_nonce_field('secure_form_action', 'secure_form_nonce');
}

    if (!isset($_POST['secure_form_nonce']) || !wp_verify_nonce($_POST['secure_form_nonce'], 'secure_form_action')) {
        wp_die('Security check failed.');
    }
}
add_action('admin_post_your_form_action', 'verify_form_nonce');
```

This snippet adds a nonce field to the form and verifies it on submission, preventing unauthorized requests.

Example 2: Limiting Failed Login Attempts
To protect against brute-force attacks, limit the number of failed login attempts.

Prompt for ChatGPT:

"Generate WordPress code to limit failed login attempts to protect against brute-force attacks."

Expected Code:

```
function limit_login_attempts($user, $username, $password) {
    $failed_attempts = get_user_meta($user->ID, 'failed_login_attempts', true) ?: 0;
```

```
    if ($failed_attempts >= 5) {
        wp_die('Too many failed login attempts. Please try
again later.');
    }

    if (!wp_check_password($password, $user->user_pass,
$user->ID)) {
        update_user_meta($user->ID, 'failed_login_attempts',
$failed_attempts + 1);
    } else {
        delete_user_meta($user->ID, 'failed_login_attempts');
    }
}
add_filter('authenticate', 'limit_login_attempts', 30, 3);
```

This code limits the number of login attempts, enhancing security against brute-force attacks.

5. AI-Driven Security Testing and Monitoring

Proactive monitoring helps catch and resolve issues before they become severe. Use AI to automate parts of this process.

Set Up Security Alerts and Monitoring

You can integrate automated alerts for critical security events like file modifications, login attempts, or server errors.

Prompt for ChatGPT:

"Suggest PHP code for WordPress to log and alert admins of unusual activity, like multiple failed login attempts or plugin file modifications."

Expected Code Example:

```
    $admin_email = get_option('admin_email');
    $subject = 'Security Alert: Unusual Activity Detected';
    $message = "Event: $event";

    wp_mail($admin_email, $subject, $message);
}


    if ($user instanceof WP_User) {
        update_user_meta($user->ID, 'failed_logins', 0);
    } else {
        $event = "Failed login attempt for username: $username";
        alert_admin_on_security_event($event);
    }
}
add_filter('authenticate', 'detect_failed_logins', 30, 3);
```

This code detects unusual login attempts and sends an email alert to the admin, keeping you informed of potential threats.

6. Summary & Key Takeaways

Here's a recap of what we covered in this chapter:
Testing and troubleshooting: Verified plugin and template functionality in a safe environment to catch errors before going live.

Optimized performance using AI-driven solutions: Addressed GTmetrix performance insights with AI-generated code for minifying assets, lazy loading, and conditional loading.

Secured the site against common vulnerabilities: Used nonce verification, limited login attempts, and AI-powered code reviews to secure your WordPress site. Monitored for security events with alerts: Created automated notifications for unusual site activity, keeping your site secure and providing peace of mind.

With your site tested, optimized, and secured, you're ready for the next chapter: Deployment and Launch. In Chapter 7,

Chapter 7: Deployment and Launch

Objective:
Successfully deploy your WordPress site, plugins, and templates from your local environment to a live server. This chapter will cover the steps to ensure a smooth and secure deployment process, best practices for going live, and tips for monitoring and maintaining your site post-launch.

1. Preparing for Deployment

Before you move your WordPress site, plugins, and templates to a live server, it's crucial to prepare by ensuring everything is error-free, optimized, and secure.
Checklist for Pre-Deployment

Final Testing in Local Environment: Revisit all plugins, shortcodes, and templates to ensure they function as expected.

Security Audit: Run a final security check. Use AI to review code for potential vulnerabilities in any custom plugins or templates (see Chapter 6).

Backup: Create a backup of your local site to preserve a working copy if anything goes wrong during deployment.

Recommended Backup Tools:

UpdraftPlus: A popular plugin that offers easy, automated backups and cloud storage options.

Duplicator: Allows you to package your entire WordPress site, including plugins and templates, for easy migration.

Tip: Use AI for Final Code Review

Run a last AI-powered review of your custom plugins and templates.

Prompt for ChatGPT:

> "Review this plugin code to ensure it follows best practices for security and performance before deployment."

2. Deploying to a Live Server

Once everything is ready, you're set to deploy your site to a live server. Here are three common ways to deploy a WordPress site from a local environment.

Option 1: Manual Migration

Best for: Smaller sites or if you're comfortable with FTP and database management.

Export Database:

Go to your local server's phpMyAdmin, select your database, and export it as an SQL file.

Upload Files:
Connect to your live server via FTP (using a client like FileZilla).
Upload your WordPress files from the local environment's wp-content folder to your live server.

Import Database:
Access phpMyAdmin on your live server, create a new database, and import the SQL file.

Update Configuration:
Update the wp-config.php file on your live server with the new database credentials.

Update URLs:
Use a plugin like Better Search Replace to replace local URLs with your live domain URLs in the database.

Option 2: Using Duplicator
Best for: Fast, easy migrations with minimal setup.

Install and Use Duplicator:
Install the Duplicator plugin on your local site.
Use the plugin to create a package, which will include your entire site and database.

Upload the Package:
Upload the Duplicator package and installer file to your live server's root directory.

Run the Installer:

Access yoursite.com/installer.php in a browser and follow the on-screen instructions to set up your site.

Option 3: Using WP Engine or Flywheel Migration Tools
Best for: Sites hosted on WP Engine or Flywheel, as they provide built-in migration tools.

Install the Migration Plugin:
Use the WP Engine or Flywheel migration plugin for an automated migration.

Follow Instructions:
Enter your credentials and follow the plugin's instructions for seamless deployment to the live server.

3. Securing the Live Site

Once deployed, it's essential to secure the live site to prevent unauthorized access or data loss.

Security Best Practices Post-Deployment

Enforce SSL:
Enable SSL on your site by installing an SSL certificate through your hosting provider. This will protect data transmitted between the server and users, especially important for forms and login pages.

Disable Directory Browsing:
Add the following line to your .htaccess file to prevent unauthorized access to site directories:

```
Options -Indexes
```

Use Two-Factor Authentication:

Install a two-factor authentication plugin, such as Two Factor Authentication by WP White Security, to add an extra layer of security.

Limit Login Attempts:

Use a plugin like Limit Login Attempts Reloaded to restrict the number of failed login attempts, preventing brute-force attacks.

Tip: Use AI to Review Security[**]

Ask ChatGPT for additional security tips specific to your setup.

Prompt for ChatGPT:

> "What additional security practices should I implement for a live WordPress site that includes custom plugins and templates?"

4. Verifying Functionality on the Live Site

After deployment, it's essential to verify that all elements function as intended on the live server.

Checklist for Functionality Testing
Check Plugins and Shortcodes:
Test all custom plugins and shortcodes to ensure they display correctly and function as expected.

Verify User Permissions:
Test different user roles to confirm that permissions are correctly set up, with sensitive features restricted to authorized users only.

Confirm Email Notifications:
If your site includes automated emails (e.g., notifications, contact forms), verify that they send properly and reach the intended recipients.

Tip: Use GTmetrix to Assess Live Performance

Run a new GTmetrix test on your live site to identify any performance issues specific to your live server environment. Address any new suggestions to ensure the site is optimized.

5. Monitoring and Maintaining Your Live Site

With your site now live, regular monitoring and maintenance are essential to ensure ongoing performance, security, and functionality.

Set Up Performance Monitoring
You can set up automated alerts for key performance indicators such as load time and server response time. Tools like UptimeRobot or Google Analytics provide valuable insights into your site's performance over time.

Automate Security Monitoring
Consider plugins like Wordfence Security or Sucuri Security for automated scanning and monitoring of potential vulnerabilities. These plugins can detect suspicious activity, such as failed login attempts or malware.

Regular Backups
Schedule regular backups of your site, including both files and the database, using a plugin like UpdraftPlus. Store backups in secure locations like Google Drive, Dropbox, or Amazon S3 to protect your data in case of a security breach or data loss.

AI for Ongoing Optimization Suggestions
Set a regular cadence for running optimization checks and using AI for performance improvements. You can prompt ChatGPT or another AI tool for updated recommendations based on your latest GTmetrix scores.

Example Prompt:

> "Analyze my GTmetrix report and suggest updated optimizations for improved performance on a live WordPress site."

6. Post-Launch Checklist

Here's a final checklist to ensure everything is functioning optimally after deployment:

SEO Setup:
Ensure that SEO plugins are configured and submit your XML sitemap to Google Search Console for indexing.

Final Security Audit:
Revisit security settings, disable any debugging modes used during development, and verify SSL status.

User Experience Testing:
Test the site's functionality across multiple devices and browsers to ensure a consistent user experience.

Sample Post-Launch Prompt for ChatGPT
Prompt:

> "Create a final post-launch checklist for a WordPress site to ensure SEO, security, and user experience are all optimized."

7. Summary & Key Takeaways

In this chapter, we covered the deployment and launch process, focusing on:
Pre-deployment preparations: Final testing, security audits, and creating backups.

Deployment methods: Manual migration, Duplicator, and automated hosting tools.
Post-launch security: Essential security steps, including SSL, two-factor authentication, and login attempt limits.
Functionality verification and performance monitoring: Ensuring all plugins, templates, and automations work as expected on the live site.
AI-driven ongoing optimization: Using AI to generate tailored suggestions for performance and security as your site grows.

Your WordPress site is now live, optimized, and secure. Congratulations on launching your first AI-assisted WordPress site! In Chapter 8: Expanding Your Skills, we'll explore advanced WordPress features, so you can continue to grow as a developer and bring even more value to your projects.
Let's keep building and learning!

This chapter provides a comprehensive guide for deploying and securing your WordPress site, including AI-driven security and optimization tips. Let me know if you're ready for Chapter 8: Expanding Your Skills or if you'd like any further customization!

Chapter 8: Expanding Your Skills

Objective:
Build on your WordPress skills by exploring advanced features, enhancing your plugins, integrating third-party APIs, and incorporating additional functionality that can elevate your development work. This chapter will introduce you to new techniques, advanced customization options, and the power of API integration.

1. Leveling Up Your Plugins with Advanced Features

Now that you've mastered creating basic plugins, let's look at some advanced techniques you can use to enhance functionality and make your plugins more powerful.

Example 1: Custom User Interfaces with WordPress Admin Pages
Custom admin pages provide a user-friendly interface for settings, reports, and plugin management within the WordPress dashboard.

Creating a Settings Page for a Plugin
Add an Admin Page: In your plugin file, add a function to create a custom settings page.

```php
function my_plugin_settings_page() {
    add_menu_page(
        'My Plugin Settings',
        'My Plugin',
        'manage_options',
        'my-plugin-settings',
        'my_plugin_render_settings_page'
    );
}
add_action('admin_menu', 'my_plugin_settings_page');

    echo '<h1>My Plugin Settings</h1>';
    echo '<form method="post" action="options.php">';
    settings_fields('my_plugin_options_group');
    do_settings_sections('my-plugin-settings');
    submit_button();
    echo '</form>';
}
```

Use AI for Custom UI Elements: Use ChatGPT to generate code for additional fields, sliders, or dropdowns, making your settings page more interactive.

Prompt:

"Generate PHP code to add a dropdown selection for greeting message styles in my WordPress plugin settings page."

Example 2: Adding Custom Post Types
Custom Post Types (CPTs) allow you to create different types of content, like portfolios, testimonials, or events.

Prompt for ChatGPT:

"Generate PHP code for a custom post type called 'Projects' with categories and tags enabled."

Expected Code:

```
    register_post_type('project', array(
        'label' => 'Projects',
        'public' => true,
        'supports' => array('title', 'editor', 'thumbnail', 'excerpt', 'comments'),
        'taxonomies' => array('category', 'post_tag')
    ));
}
add_action('init', 'my_plugin_register_post_type');
```

Explanation: This code registers a new custom post type "Projects," allowing you to categorize and tag project posts.

2. Integrating Third-Party APIs for Dynamic Data

APIs allow you to pull in data from external sources to add real-time functionality to your WordPress plugins or templates.

Example: Displaying Real-Time Weather Data
Using an API like OpenWeatherMap, you can create a widget that displays the current weather based on the visitor's location.

Step 1: Get API Access
Sign up for an API key at , which provides weather data through a simple API request.

Step 2: Generate Code with AI

Prompt for ChatGPT:

> "Generate a WordPress widget that displays current weather information using the OpenWeatherMap API."

Expected Code:

```
class Weather_Widget extends WP_Widget {

        parent::__construct('weather_widget', 'Weather
Widget', array('description' => 'Displays current
weather.'));
    }


        $apiKey = 'YOUR_API_KEY';
        $location = 'London';
        $weather_data =
file_get_contents("https://api.openweathermap.org/data/2.5/we
ather?q={$location}&appid={$apiKey}&units=metric");
        $weather = json_decode($weather_data);

        echo $args['before_widget'];
        echo "<h2>Weather in {$location}</h2>";
        echo "<p>Temperature: " . $weather->main->temp .
"°C</p>";
        echo "<p>Condition: " . $weather->weather[0]-
>description . "</p>";
        echo $args['after_widget'];
    }
}
add_action('widgets_init', function() {
    register_widget('Weather_Widget');
});
```

Explanation: This code creates a widget that displays weather information for a specific location. You can use this as a base and customize it to dynamically detect the user's location.

3. Using AI for Advanced Customizations and Conditional Logic

AI can generate custom code snippets to help you create more advanced, user-friendly experiences in WordPress.

Example 1: Conditional Content Based on User Role
Use conditional logic to display different content depending on the user's role.

Prompt for ChatGPT:

> "Generate code to display a custom message only for administrators on the WordPress dashboard."

Expected Code:

```
if (current_user_can('administrator')) {
        echo '<div class="notice notice-success"><p>Welcome, Admin! Here are your latest updates.</p></div>';
    }
}
add_action('admin_notices', 'admin_only_message');
```

Explanation: This code adds a message visible only to administrators on the WordPress dashboard, enhancing targeted user experience.

Example 2: Conditional Display of Plugins or Templates

You may want certain plugins or templates to behave differently based on specific conditions, like time of day, location, or user preferences.

Prompt for ChatGPT:

"Generate PHP code to load a custom CSS style only on the homepage and only during the evening hours."

Expected Code:

```
if (is_front_page() && date("H") >= 18) {
    wp_enqueue_style('evening-style',
get_template_directory_uri() . '/css/evening.css');
    }
}
add_action('wp_enqueue_scripts', 'evening_style');
```

Explanation: This code conditionally loads a CSS file for the homepage in the evening, offering a unique visual experience based on time.

4. Enhancing Site Speed and Security with Advanced Techniques

As your site grows, maintaining speed and security becomes even more important. Here are some advanced AI-driven optimization and security techniques to consider.

AI-Driven Performance Optimization

AI can assist in more sophisticated optimization strategies like database indexing, caching, and optimizing JavaScript.

Prompt for ChatGPT:

> "Generate code to add caching for database queries in a WordPress plugin to improve performance."

Expected Code:

```
$transient_name = 'cached_posts';
    $cached_posts = get_transient($transient_name);

    if ($cached_posts === false) {
        $cached_posts = new WP_Query(array('posts_per_page' => 5));
        set_transient($transient_name, $cached_posts, HOUR_IN_SECONDS);
    }

    return $cached_posts;
}
```

Explanation: This code caches the result of a query for one hour, reducing the number of database requests and improving site performance.

Enhanced Security with AI Assistance

Use AI for in-depth security checks, encryption techniques, and proactive vulnerability assessments.

Example Prompt for Security Hardening:

> "Review this WordPress plugin code for potential security vulnerabilities, and suggest ways to harden the plugin against XSS and SQL injection."

ChatGPT can provide tailored advice and code snippets to secure forms, sanitize inputs, and escape outputs, helping to prevent attacks.

5. Exploring Next-Level Functionality with WordPress REST API

The WordPress REST API allows for powerful integrations and customizations by enabling data retrieval and updates through external applications.
Example: Displaying WordPress Data on a Non-WordPress Site
With the REST API, you can pull data from your WordPress site and display it on a separate site or application.

Enable REST API Access: The REST API is enabled by default in WordPress; however, you may need authentication for private data.

Fetch Data Using the REST API:
Use the following URL to fetch recent posts: https://yoursite.com/wp-json/wp/v2/posts

Display Data on an External Site:
Use JavaScript or a backend language to fetch and display data.

```
    .then(response => response.json())
    .then(posts => {
        posts.forEach(post => {
            console.log(`Title: ${post.title.rendered}`);
```

```
    });
});
```

Explanation: This JavaScript fetches posts from the WordPress REST API, making it easy to integrate WordPress content into non-WordPress environments.

6. Summary & Key Takeaways

This chapter covered advanced skills and techniques that will help you expand your capabilities as a WordPress developer:

Enhanced Plugin Functionality: You explored custom settings pages, custom post types, and conditional content displays for greater control and customization.

Third-Party API Integration: Integrated external data, like weather information, into your plugins or templates for dynamic and interactive features. Performance and Security Best Practices: Leveraged AI for caching, query optimization, and security hardening.

Using the WordPress REST API: Accessed WordPress data externally, allowing for powerful integrations and advanced customizations.
In the next chapter, Chapter 9: Improving Site Performance and SEO, we'll dive deeper into speed optimization and SEO best practices to ensure your site is fast, visible, and ready to attract an audience.

Let's continue building and fine-tuning your WordPress skills!

This chapter introduces advanced WordPress techniques, practical examples, and AI-driven enhancements, providing a solid foundation for expanding your development expertise. Let me know if you're ready for Chapter 9 or if you need any further customization!

Chapter 9: Improving Site Performance and SEO

Objective:
Optimize your WordPress site to load quickly and rank well on search engines. This chapter will guide you through essential SEO practices, performance optimization techniques, and advanced AI-driven strategies to boost site speed and visibility.

1. Understanding the Importance of Performance and SEO

A well-optimized site provides a better user experience, lowers bounce rates, and improves conversions. SEO, on the other hand, helps bring organic traffic by making your site visible to users searching for relevant content. Together, performance and SEO ensure that your site is fast, visible, and impactful.

Key Areas to Focus On:

Page Speed Optimization: Improve load times to enhance the user experience and SEO.

Core Web Vitals: Focus on metrics like Largest Contentful Paint (LCP), First Input Delay (FID), and Cumulative Layout Shift (CLS), which Google considers for ranking.

On-Page SEO: Optimize content, metadata, and images for search engines.

2. Using GTmetrix and PageSpeed Insights for Speed Optimization

GTmetrix and PageSpeed Insights offer detailed insights into site performance, helping you pinpoint areas for improvement.

Step 1: Run a Performance Test

GTmetrix: Go to , run a test on your site, and review the performance metrics.

Google PageSpeed Insights: Visit PageSpeed Insights to get Google's perspective on your site's performance.

Focus on areas such as image optimization, JavaScript minification, and render-blocking resources.

Step 2: Use AI to Address Optimization Suggestions
Example Prompts for AI Optimization:
Image Optimization:
"Generate code for a WordPress plugin that automatically compresses and resizes images upon upload to improve site speed."

Expected Code:

```
function optimize_image_upload($file) {
    if (strpos($file['type'], 'image') !== false) {
        $image_editor = wp_get_image_editor($file['tmp_name']);
        if (!is_wp_error($image_editor)) {
            $image_editor->set_quality(80);
            $image_editor->resize(1200, 800, true); // Adjust dimensions as needed
            $image_editor->save($file['tmp_name']);
        }
    }
    return $file;
}
add_filter('wp_handle_upload_prefilter', 'optimize_image_upload');
```

Minifying JavaScript and CSS:

> "Create a WordPress plugin that minifies JavaScript and CSS files to reduce page load time."

3. Core Web Vitals: Optimizing Key Metrics for SEO

Google's Core Web Vitals—LCP, FID, and CLS—are crucial for ranking.

Here's how to improve each:

Largest Contentful Paint (LCP)

LCP measures the time it takes for the main content to load. Improving LCP involves reducing image sizes, minimizing CSS and JavaScript, and ensuring fast server response times.

Lazy Load Images: Only load images when they're about to enter the viewport.
Optimize CSS: Use AI to help minify CSS and avoid blocking the main content.

Prompt for Lazy Loading:
"Generate JavaScript code to lazy load images on a WordPress site to improve LCP."

Expected Code:

```
document.addEventListener("DOMContentLoaded", function() {
    const images = document.querySelectorAll("img");
    images.forEach(img => {
        img.setAttribute("loading", "lazy");
    });
});
```

First Input Delay (FID)
FID measures the time from when a user first interacts with the page to when the browser responds. Improve FID by optimizing JavaScript execution and reducing long tasks.

Minimize JavaScript Execution: Use asynchronous loading for scripts.

Use AI to Optimize Code: For example, prompt ChatGPT to identify parts of JavaScript that could be refactored for efficiency.

Cumulative Layout Shift (CLS)
CLS measures visual stability, quantifying how much content shifts during load. Fix CLS by setting dimensions for images and videos and avoiding dynamically injected content above the fold.

Define Size Attributes: Ensure all media elements have width and height set in CSS.

AI-Assisted Code Review for CLS prompt:

> "Review this CSS to ensure it prevents layout shifts, specifically for images and embedded videos."

4. On-Page SEO Optimization

Effective on-page SEO helps search engines understand and rank your content better. Here's how to use AI for optimized titles, meta descriptions, and structured content.

AI-Generated Meta Titles and Descriptions
Use AI to create engaging and keyword-rich meta titles and descriptions for each page.

Prompt for ChatGPT:

> "Generate a meta title and description for a WordPress blog post about 'The Benefits of AI in Web Development.'"

Expected AI Output:

> Meta Title: "The Benefits of AI in Web Development: Boosting Productivity and Innovation"
>
> Meta Description: "Discover how AI is transforming web development, from code generation to performance optimization. Learn how to leverage AI tools to create better websites faster."

Structuring Content with AI

AI can also help create structured content that's more SEO-friendly. Use AI to generate H2 and H3 subheadings for a blog post or product page.

Prompt for ChatGPT:

> "Create an outline with H2 and H3 subheadings for a blog post titled 'Top 10 SEO Strategies for WordPress Sites.'"

Expected Outline:

> H2: Introduction to WordPress SEO
> H2: Optimizing Page Speed
> H3: Minifying CSS and JavaScript
> H3: Lazy Loading Images
> H2: Improving Content Structure
> H3: Using Headings and Subheadings
> H3: Adding Internal Links

5. Image Optimization for SEO and Performance

Images are essential for user engagement but can slow down your site if not optimized. Here's how to handle images for both SEO and speed.

Use AI to Generate ALT Text for Images

ALT text helps with accessibility and image SEO. Prompt ChatGPT to generate descriptive ALT text for various images.

Prompt for ChatGPT:

"Generate ALT text for an image of a sunset over a city skyline."

Expected AI Output:
"Sunset over a city skyline with orange and purple hues filling the sky."

Automate Image Compression and Conversion
Compress images and convert them to WebP format for faster loading without compromising quality.

Example Plugin for WebP Conversion:

Prompt for ChatGPT:

"Generate code for a WordPress plugin that converts uploaded images to WebP format and compresses them for optimal performance."

Expected Code:

```
function convert_to_webp($file) {
    if (strpos($file['type'], 'image') !== false) {
        $image = wp_get_image_editor($file['tmp_name']);
        if (!is_wp_error($image)) {
            $image->save($file['tmp_name'], 'image/webp');
        }
    }
    return $file;
}
add_filter('wp_handle_upload', 'convert_to_webp');
```

6. Advanced SEO with Schema Markup

Schema markup, or structured data, helps search engines understand your content more precisely, potentially leading to rich snippets in search results.

Adding Basic Schema Markup
Add schema markup to posts, especially for reviews, events, or product pages.

Prompt for ChatGPT:
"Generate JSON-LD schema markup for a blog post with the title 'How to Improve WordPress SEO' and author 'João Castro'."

Expected Schema Markup:

```
<script type="application/ld+json">
{
    "@context": "http://schema.org",
    "@type": "BlogPosting",
    "headline": "How to Improve WordPress SEO",
    "author": {
        "@type": "Person",
        "name": "João Castro"
    },
    "publisher": {
        "@type": "Organization",
        "name": "Your Blog Name",
        "logo": {
            "@type": "ImageObject",
            "url": "https://yourblog.com/logo.png"
        }
    },
    "datePublished": "2024-11-15"
}
</script>
```

Explanation: Add this JSON-LD code in the header of the specific post for enhanced SEO.

7. Leveraging AI to Continuously Improve SEO and Performance

Use AI to keep up with SEO and performance trends. Here are some useful prompts to automate ongoing improvements.

Content Refresh:
Prompt: "List 5 ways to refresh content on a WordPress blog post about 'Web Development Trends.'"

Use ChatGPT suggestions to regularly update your content for relevance.

Keyword Suggestions:
Prompt:

> "Suggest long-tail keywords related to 'AI in WordPress Development.'"

Integrate these keywords into your content, headings, and meta tags for better SEO performance.

SEO Audits:

> Prompt: "Perform an SEO audit on a WordPress site focusing on meta tags, headings, and internal links."

Implement AI-generated suggestions for a thorough SEO cleanup.

8. Summary & Key Takeaways

This chapter provided a comprehensive approach to optimizing your WordPress site for both speed and SEO, including AI-driven enhancements:
GTmetrix and **PageSpeed Insights**: Leveraged these tools to identify areas for performance improvement and used AI to generate code solutions.
Core Web Vitals: Focused on improving LCP, FID, and CLS with AI-generated optimizations.
On-Page SEO: Used AI to generate meta descriptions, ALT text, and structured outlines for SEO-optimized content.
Schema Markup: Added structured data to improve search visibility and chances for rich snippets.

In Chapter 10: Easy Deployment and Maintenance (with Video Guide), we'll cover final deployment steps and practical maintenance tips to keep your WordPress site running smoothly. Let's continue building a high-performance, SEO-friendly site that's ready to succeed in search engines and user experience!

This chapter balances technical SEO and performance improvements with accessible, AI-driven enhancements. Let me know if you'd like to proceed to Chapter 10 or if you need any further customization!

Chapter 10: Easy Deployment and Maintenance

Objective:
Deploy your optimized WordPress site and set up an easy-to-follow maintenance routine. This chapter covers final deployment steps, automation tools, and best practices for maintaining a fast, secure, and user-friendly site.

1. The Importance of Deployment and Maintenance

Proper deployment ensures your WordPress site launches smoothly, with all elements functioning as intended. Maintenance is equally crucial, as it helps keep your site fast, secure, and error-free over time. This chapter will guide you through deploying your site effectively and establishing a streamlined maintenance routine that you can follow to keep your site in top shape.

2. Finalizing Deployment with Ease

You're ready to go live! Here's a quick checklist and some options to deploy your site efficiently.

Pre-Deployment Checklist
Backup the Site: Ensure you have a full backup, including the database and all files. Use plugins like UpdraftPlus or All-in-One WP Migration to make the process quick and reliable.

Final Testing: Re-check plugins, shortcodes, and any user-facing elements on a staging environment to ensure everything works as expected.

Security and Performance Audit: Run final security checks and performance tests on GTmetrix or PageSpeed Insights to verify site readiness.

Deployment Options
There are multiple ways to deploy a WordPress site; choose the method that best fits your setup.

Manual Deployment (FTP): For control over every file, manually upload files via FTP to your server. Import your database via phpMyAdmin and adjust the wp-config.php file with live server credentials.

Using Duplicator for Simplified Deployment:
Duplicator is a plugin that packages your WordPress site into a single file for easy migration.
After creating a package, upload it to the live server and run the Duplicator installer to set up the site.

Managed Hosting Deployments: Many managed WordPress hosts like WP Engine and Flywheel offer one-click deployment from staging to production.

3. Essential Maintenance Practices

Once live, maintaining your WordPress site is key to its ongoing performance, security, and reliability. Here's how to set up a simple, effective maintenance routine.

Automate Backups
Automated backups ensure that you always have a recent copy of your site in case of an emergency.

UpdraftPlus: Set up daily or weekly backups of your files and database. Store backups in a remote location like Google Drive or Dropbox for added security.
Jetpack: Jetpack's premium plan includes real-time backups, ideal for sites with frequent updates.

Update WordPress, Plugins, and Themes
Outdated plugins and themes are common vulnerabilities. Automate updates where possible and set reminders for manual checks.

Automate Core Updates:
WordPress automatically installs minor updates, but major updates may require manual action.

Prompt for ChatGPT:

"Generate PHP code to automate major WordPress updates for plugins and themes."

Expected php Code:

```
add_filter('auto_update_plugin', '__return_true');
add_filter('auto_update_theme', '__return_true');
```

Monthly Manual Checks: Schedule a reminder to manually check compatibility and functionality after updates, especially for custom plugins and themes.

4. Monitoring Site Security and Performance

Monitoring ensures that your site remains secure and performs optimally. Use both plugins and AI for ongoing maintenance.

Set Up Security Monitoring

Wordfence Security: This plugin offers comprehensive security features, including firewall protection, malware scanning, and real-time traffic monitoring.

Sucuri Security: Sucuri provides a full suite of security options, including audit logs, file integrity monitoring, and DDoS protection.
Prompt for AI Assistance:

> "Provide tips to harden WordPress security using Wordfence and additional PHP code for custom security alerts."

Performance Monitoring with UptimeRobot

Automate Uptime Monitoring: UptimeRobot notifies you if your site goes offline, helping you stay ahead of potential issues.

Set Up Weekly Performance Checks: Use GTmetrix or PageSpeed Insights for weekly performance audits to catch issues early.

Sample Prompt for AI-Assisted Maintenance:

> "List five maintenance tasks I should check weekly to keep my WordPress site optimized and secure."

Expected AI Suggestions:

> Verify that all plugins and themes are updated.
> Check GTmetrix for any new performance issues.
> Review Wordfence logs for security alerts.
> Ensure recent backups are intact and stored remotely.

Test contact forms and interactive elements for functionality.

5. Automating Content Updates and SEO Maintenance

Regular updates keep your site fresh and SEO-friendly. Use automation to streamline these updates.

Scheduled Content Updates
Automate blog posts, seasonal updates, or promotional messages with scheduling tools and plugins.

WP Scheduled Posts: Schedule posts and content updates in advance.
Use AI for Content Refresh Ideas: Generate new ideas to keep content fresh with ChatGPT.

Prompt for Content Update Suggestions:

> "Suggest seasonal blog topics for a WordPress site about web development and tech trends."

SEO Maintenance with Yoast SEO
Automate SEO Checks: Use the Yoast SEO plugin to ensure pages meet SEO guidelines and keep your XML sitemap updated.
Monthly SEO Audits: Run an SEO audit using tools like Ahrefs or Google Search Console for insights on ranking, broken links, and search visibility.

6. Handling Common Maintenance Issues with AI Assistance

Common issues include broken links, plugin conflicts, and performance drops. AI can assist with troubleshooting and suggesting quick fixes.

Broken Link Fixes

Broken links can negatively impact user experience and SEO. Use a plugin like Broken Link Checker or ask AI for help.

Prompt for ChatGPT:

> "Provide PHP code to check for broken links within WordPress posts and pages."

Expected Code:

```
    preg_match_all('/<a href="([^"]*)"/', $content, $matches);
    $broken_links = array();
    foreach ($matches[1] as $link) {
        $response = wp_remote_get($link);
        if (is_wp_error($response) || wp_remote_retrieve_response_code($response) != 200) {
            $broken_links[] = $link;
        }
    }
    return $broken_links;
}
```

AI for Resolving Plugin Conflicts

If plugins conflict, use AI to suggest alternative plugins or fixes.

Prompt for ChatGPT:

"Suggest solutions for plugin conflicts in WordPress, specifically when both plugins modify the same shortcode."

Expected Response:

```
Adjust the shortcode names to be unique for each plugin.
Use conditional checks in the functions.php file to disable
specific plugins on certain pages.
```

7. Video Guide: Deploying and Maintaining Your Site

Provide a special video walkthrough for readers, showing them how to:
Deploy the Site: Demonstrate deployment using Duplicator or a similar tool.
Set Up Automated Maintenance: Guide users through automating backups, updates, and security monitoring.

Monthly Maintenance Routine: Cover essential tasks like checking GTmetrix, running Wordfence scans, and reviewing content.

This video is a companion resource to make these steps easier to follow and helps reinforce the maintenance routine outlined in this chapter.

8. Summary & Key Takeaways

This chapter covered the essential steps for deploying and maintaining your WordPress site:

Deployment Methods: Provided options for manual deployment, Duplicator, and managed hosting.
Automated Backups and Updates: Set up automatic backups and updates to ensure security and stability.

Security and Performance Monitoring: Used tools like Wordfence, Sucuri, and UptimeRobot to keep your site safe and responsive.

Automating Content and SEO Maintenance: Scheduled content updates, SEO checks, and monthly audits for a consistently fresh and optimized site.

With these skills, you're well-prepared to keep your site in top shape, providing visitors with a fast, secure, and engaging experience. Congratulations on reaching the end of 1% Developer, 99% Idiot!. Your journey as an AI-powered WordPress creator has only just begun, and this foundation will serve you well in creating innovative web solutions.

Thank you for taking this journey with me—now go forth and create something amazing!

www.ingramcontent.com/pod-product-compliance
Lightning Source LLC
Chambersburg PA
CBHW070117230526
45472CB00004B/1305